Mom,
I hope you enjoy the
book as much as we
enjoyed your visit—
Happy Mothers Day
Mick & Maureen
'98

Photography By N. Jane Iseley

Text By William P. Baldwin III

CHARLESTON

Legacy Publications

A Subsidiary of Pace Communications, Inc.
Greensboro, North Carolina

PHOTOGRAPHY © 1997 / *N. Jane Iseley*

*I'd like to thank the residents of Charleston for graciously sharing their city
with us, especialy Dot and Horry Kerrison. Also, my friends at Legacy Publications, David Brown,
Bob Hudson, Bonnie McElveen-Hunter, Patsy McConnell, Barry Mayberry, and Shelia Rooker.*

TEXT © 1997 / *William P. Baldwin III*

*I'd like to thank Alex Moore for editing and Dr. George Rogers for inspiration.
And for coffee, conversation, and guidance, a particular thanks to Jose Caban, Mary Giles,
David Moltke-Hansen, Charles DeAntonio, David Boatwright, Steve Hoffius,
Mary Pope Waring, Lucia Jaycocks, Emily Whaley, Mary Legare, and Cynthia Jenkins.*

DESIGN / *Jaimey Easler, Palmetto Graphic Design Company*

EDITOR / *Sheryl Krieger Miller*

PROOFREADER / *Carol Stearns Medford*

PHOTOGRAPHY COORDINATIOR / *Alice Turner Michalak*

ISBN / 0-933101-17-1 *(Hard Bound)*

ISBN / 0-933101-18-X *(Soft Bound)*

LIBRARY OF CONGRESS CATALOG CARD NUMBER / 97-74350

PREPRESS / *NEC Color 4, Nashville, Tennessee*

PRINTING / *Friesens, Altona, Manitoba, Canada*

INTRODUCTION / *Charleston is a welcoming place. "The people are vastly affable and polite," wrote an 18th-century visitor. The tradition continues today. Charleston was chosen America's friendliest city for the second year in a row.* ❧ *Hospitality, simple manners—those courtesies that soften life's bumpy journey—are indeed a Charleston institution. "Pleases" and "thank yous" and nods and waves are the norm. People aren't in a hurry—even if they should be. Meals are leisurely affairs. People walk where they're going. Charleston is truly a pedestrian city. It's walkable. Livable. Visitable. Welcome.* ❧ *Now consider this. Charleston is a construction of sights and sounds,*

THE MAP

From a Survey of the Coast of the United States, 1866—a rare "Union" look at the City.

tastes and smells and textures. A blaze of azalea blossoms. A cobbling of cobblestones and a patch of peeling stucco. Sunlight, both bright and dappled, and violet shadows. She-crab soup in a blue willow bowl. Shrimp and grits. Stately church bells pealing, piercing gulls' cries, and pure silence. "The sensuous city," historian George Rogers calls it and wonders half jokingly if the events of history have left "a glamor that enhances the senses." Can we actually "feel" history? Or more to

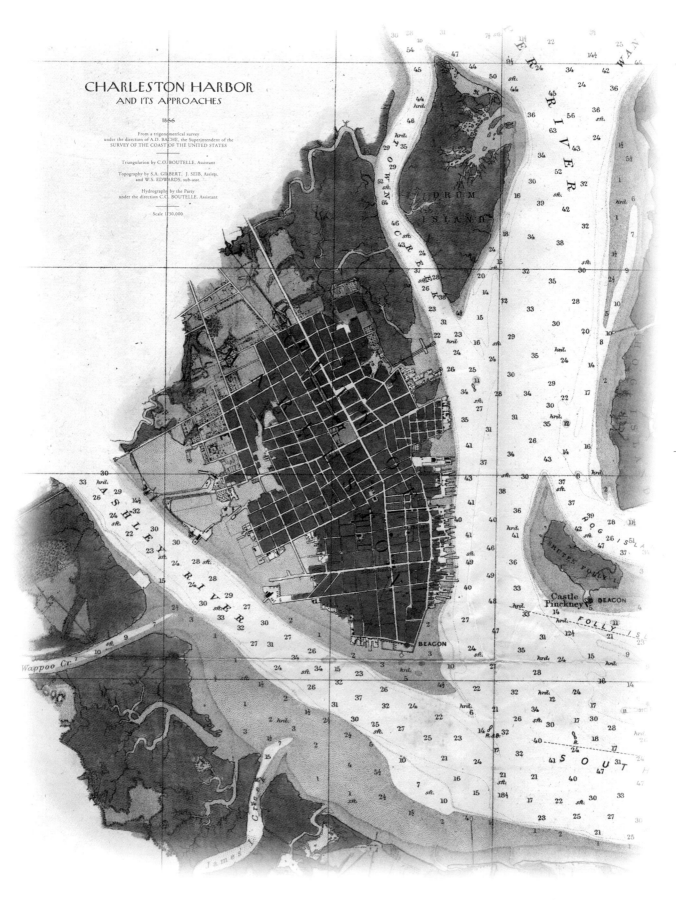

CHARLESTON HARBOR
AND ITS APPROACHES

1866

From a trigonometrical survey
under the direction of A.D. BACHE, the Superintendent of the
SURVEY OF THE COAST OF THE UNITED STATES

Triangulation by C.O. BOUTELLE, Assistant

Topography by S.A. GILBERT, J. SEIB, Assists.
and W.S. EDWARDS, sub-asst.

Hydrography by the Party
under the direction C.C. BOUTELLE, Assistant

Scale 1/30.000

the point, do we want to? ❦ Certainly enough facts exist to support the romantic vision of an aristocrats' city, one of architectural grandeur and a festive, genteel society enriched by art and learning. In her Golden Age before the Revolution, Charleston was the premier city of the South—unsurpassed in wealth and learning, the arbiter of all fashion. ❦ Her political leaders were

statesmen—technically, at least, this country's first "president" was Charleston merchant, Henry Laurens, presiding officer at the Continental Congress when the Declaration of Independence was signed. Books mattered. Charleston had the first lending library. Education was valued. Though some planters sent their sons off to England, the town had several free and many paid schools. There were churches of practically every denomination. And a synagogue. And theaters. A bawdy farce titled *The Recruiting Officer* played here in 1736 to a wildly enthusiastic audience. Coaches and horses were imported—despite claims that even better ones could be obtained locally. Tailors, wig makers, and milliners kept up with the latest English styles and stitched and powdered accordingly. And lessons were given in dance and music, for these were the town's passions. Charleston furniture makers copied European craftsmen who were not necessarily their betters. Mansions were built and fine gardens established. And following the Revolution, in what some see as a period of cultural decline, a great burst of both private and public building began. Horse races and grand balls and banquets continued. Portrait painters were in demand, and we can view the results at the Gibbes Museum of Art. Even the fatal coming of the Civil War held its romantic charm—one marked by the stoic bravery of both men and women. All of this is a realistic part of Charleston's "Gone with the Wind" heritage. ❦ Yes, we have reminders before us. Examine the opulent interiors of the five main museum houses—spiraling staircases and a mirror windowed music room. Or visit the tremendous gardens located just beyond the city's edge. Charleston does indeed enjoy a distinctive and glamorous pedigree. ❦ Having said that, it's still doubtful that many of us would have chosen to live here in centuries past. Disease and death were

PORTRAIT IN CITY HALL

The "Fire Masters" took a "Dutch Masters" pose for this 1841 portrait by Christian Mayo.

everyday occurrences. Mosquitoes, heat, and calamity were as well. Often the city was both a fortress and a graveyard. The roads were either dusty or boggy, and even in the best of times, the gutter smells were awful. Poorer whites felt disenfranchised, which they were. And all whites lived in continual fear of the black slaves who lived in fear of them. Friendliness aside, beneath the most innocent social transactions was a layer of mistrust, and in the people, a propensity for violence. ⁂ The city of then is not the city of now. Fortunately. And yet they are the same. We can still walk streets that are largely untouched over the last 100 and sometimes 200 years. And the buildings crowding in on us are not fanciful reconstructions but originals. Seventy-three Charleston structures date from before the Revolution and 789 more are antebellum. We are indeed sauntering where pirates sauntered. The Swamp Fox, General Francis Marion, leaped from one Charleston balcony and General George Washington spoke from another. Cannonballs whistled through the oak branches—and the attics. Duels were fought on these small greens. Courtships were pressed and war conducted and reels danced. And life was lived. Extravagantly by a few. Humbly by most. Charleston was not just a town of aristocratic splendor, wealth, and privilege. You will see ample evidence of the other Charleston. And perhaps in some mystical way all of this collective "living" has left a "glamor" behind, a patina of history that does "enhance the senses." If so, then all we need is a bit of imagination—the sympathetic kind the poets use—and the city is ours to enjoy.

A VERY, VERY SHORT HISTORY / *Charleston was founded in 1670 at nearby "Old Town Plantation" and 10 years later moved to the peninsula between the Cooper and Ashley rivers—a site easier to*

defend and far more convenient to the harbor. The colony was under the direction of Lord Ashley Cooper (hence the rivers' names) and seven other Lord Proprietors, powerful friends of King Charles II, who had received the colony as a gift and expected riches from her. The settlers had their own agenda and turned quickly to making their fortunes, first with an Indian trade in deer hides and the manufacture of ship stores. Experiments with "plantation" crops soon followed. Rice and indigo proved profitable and so, unfortunately, slavery proved profitable as well. Religious tolerance brought a wide collection of dissenting faiths, and the "Holy City's" first churches were built. Indians were subdued as were the pirates and the Spanish. And the Charleston-based planters and merchants worked out their common destiny, deposing first the Proprietors (1719) and then the King's men (1776). ❧ We can see this for ourselves. The Charleston Museum has handsome displays. The Old Powder Magazine is a museum dedicated to this earlier period. We can visit Fort Moultrie, the site of

a memorable Revolutionary War victory, or the Exchange Building and its dungeon exhibits. Or the Unitarian Church, where an explosion threw civilian bodies against the wall. Leaders Rutledge, Pinckney, Laurens, and Gadsden gave their names to streets. ❧ Following the Revolution, cotton brought even grander wealth, more slaves, and a growing insulation to Charleston, for the world's censure and the threat of slave revolt turned the city ever inward. The Denmark Vesey uprising of 1822 caused the original Citadel to be built and caused the long spikes, the "chevaux-de-frise," to be placed atop fences and gates. The Old Slave Mart is still here and so is Vesey's house. ❧ John C. Calhoun, commemorated in statue and tomb, defended the status quo while others clamored for another rebellion that finally came in 1861. Fort Sumter was fired upon, and the Union fired back until Charleston was brought to her knees and the slaves freed. Perhaps this was the city's opportunity to enter the modern age. We have the Avery Institute to remind us of the black community's hopes and an occasional Victorian mansion to suggest prosperity. However, economic hardship followed. ❧ Charleston remained frozen. Many would say fortunately so—at least in the currency of nostalgia this was Charleston's true "Golden Age"—a time of 3 o'clock dinners and "the living is easy." The Jenkins Orphanage band gave the Charleston dance craze to the world, and a "Renaissance" in literature and the arts occurred. Except for the addition of a Naval shipyard, Charleston had few financial resources—until tourism rescued her in the 1930s. Outside dollars spurred the restoration, which in turn brought in even more visitors. The city entered a self-perpetuating revitalization and boom.

CITADEL PARADE

In 1842, the S.C. Military Academy, known as the Citadel, began to offer "a broad and practical education."

THE SHAPE OF THINGS / *Charleston has a skyline sculpted by fire, hurricane, earthquake, and cannonball. What you see is the result of humanity proposing and God disposing, of planning and not* planning … and Charleston rising from the ashes (or muddy water) like a phoenix. You'll notice only an occasional church steeple aspires to more than three or four stories, which in the end makes for a very human scale—a comfortable proportion of humanity to structures, with green trees filling up the cracks between, and streets, lanes, and alleys webbing it together. ⁂ In the beginning, the Lord Proprietors provided the city with a plan, "the Grand Modell." Today's Broad, Meeting, and East Bay streets were laid out as wide straight avenues with a large town square where Broad and Meeting crossed—today's "Four Corners of the Law." Unfortunately, the city's first defensive wall was to enclose an area only four blocks long and two blocks wide with a drawbridge separating the planned square. In addition, the settlement of Colonel William Rhett's plantation on the western boundary meant that the main entry road was pushed to the narrower King Street. Bounded on three sides by marsh and rivers, land was at a premium. Property owners allowed only the narrowest of accesses when subdividing their land, some arguing that the crowded buildings offered shade and coolness. A typical cityscape put houses hard against the sidewalk. ⁂ Right angles for roads were abandoned as well. The course of creeks that spread like fingers into the high land dictated curious slants and bends like those found on Church Street and Zig Zag Alley. Indeed, some creeks would eventually become roads themselves. Water Street is one, and Market is another.

NAMES / *And adding to this confusion are the names. "The names of Charleston streets are often changed and hardly ever to the better,"* *wrote John Bennett. King Street was originally the Broad Path. Church* was New Church because the original Church Street became Meeting Street after the Presbyterian meeting house located there. Chalmers was the street John Bennett had in mind—its reputation for liquor and loose women had made it a disreputable address to claim and a change from Union Alley was considered a partial corrective. ⁂ Indeed, the city as a port and lively sporting center would from its beginnings support what in this century were finally labeled as "zones of vice." As marshlands became filled and the constricting fortifications were abandoned, new and fashionable suburbs would leapfrog over these rowdy districts and earlier decaying neighborhoods and through the changes of fortune fall into disrepair themselves and be abandoned—and then resurrected. And the same in miniature occurred as individual lots were subdivided or combined. In short, it's possible to see the city as an organism— sick, well, up and down, expanding, contracting, and strangely alive.

THE PORT / *"Sea drinking city" and "Stainless maid to the ocean," poets have called Charleston, for she was first and foremost a port. In the beginning, a modest sea wall and two cannon-armed batteries defended*

the colonists from hurricanes and foreign invaders. One of these structures would eventually be extended and raised and extended and raised numerous times until we have the present "Battery." The other had the Exchange Building built upon it. Wharfs, sometimes called bridges, went out through the marsh to the rivers, but much of that area is filled in as well. Shops with lodging above lined the waterfront as did more of those taverns where a sailor might "wrap his lips around a pewter engine." But the advent of steam and the increase in ship size would make the harbor obsolete and bring economic hardship. The city looked landward to a canal and railroad for help. Defensive walls had already come down, and Charlestonians pushed toward "the Out." Charleston was quite literally a melting pot—bubbling over.

THE PEOPLE / *This city, like any other in America, is a city of immigrants. The numerous social organizations, the elite societies with their guarded membership, were originally organized to ease the*

burden of newly arriving fellow countrymen. We often hear of the English, the Barbadians, and the Huguenot French, but antebellum Charleston was also home to Jews, Italians, Irish, Scots, French Catholics, and Germans— and most significant of all, enslaved Africans. And yes, even Yankees. Following the Revolution, Yankee merchants literally colonized the city mercantile establishment. ✥ This collection of citizenry was a heady mixture, one that made possible the rich cultural life that is now being preserved and celebrated, but was also the source of conflict. Planters wanted the city for a summer retreat, a place to enjoy "Society" and be free of the country fevers. Merchants wanted commercial expansion as well as their urban estates. And the new arrivals were pushing up, keeping shop and practicing crafts and competing against slaves who were, of course, struggling to improve their own lot. And all of these together left behind a vivid record—one partly recorded in brick and timber.

ARCHITECTURE / *Architectural styles are a product most often of fashion, technology, and need. And happily for us, Charlestonians enjoyed a finely tuned sense of all three. For affluent residences, this*

usually meant a handsome rendering of traditional styles, but for much else, especially public buildings, they indulged a penchant for the "modern" or at least most fashionable. ✥ What's built before the Revolution is known as Georgian, as in the King Georges. The very earliest of these tend to be low, small, solid buildings with steep medieval roofs (the Pink House), soon followed by two-story rectangles with shallow hipped roofs (much of Church Street), and the even more substantial "double houses" and heavy columned Palladian mansions (Miles Brewton Home). Next came the Federal period, with a democratic adjustment—the fine-lined influence of the Adams Brothers. Lighter and more intricate decoration is the hallmark, with amateur architect Gabriel Manigault as the chief exponent (Joseph Manigault house). By the 1820s, Greek Revival or Neoclassical was introduced by America's first native-born professional architect Robert Mills leading the way, and grand columned "temples" lined the streets both narrow and broad. Then E.B. White and the partnership of Frances D. Lee and Edward C. Jones introduced the more exotic revivals—Italianate with its bracketed embellishment, the arched and crenellated toppings of Gothic, and even the dreamscape arches of the Moorish. All were preferable, argued critics like William Gilmore Simms, to Greek temples meant to be situated on Greek hilltops. And "Victorianization" followed after the Civil War, giving us a handful of grand mansard roof mansions and some much-gabled Queen Anne bungalows. Then

Charleston's architectural progression comes pretty much to a halt—except for the business district's stores, an eclectic collection that is just now being fully appreciated. ❧ But this helpful categorizing can't always be applied. To begin with, we must consider Charleston's wonderful single house, which is not so much an architectural style as a homegrown attitude

toward living: narrow houses, turned gable end to the street. One room wide and two deep with another story or two above, they were being built here by the 1740s. Then sometime before the Revolution double piazzas began to grace the long sides and were almost always present in the 1800s. ❧ Theories abound as to why the single house should prove so popular. Taxes at one time were based on the street-side windows. And fires did leap easily between connected houses. But the most probable cause is that such houses, especially with their balconies, catch the breezes. Architectural historian Sam Stoney explains: "Its prime reason for being as it is, is the sacred Charleston wind that every hot afternoon blows up from the southwest across the Ashley River and cools off the town for the evening. Notice and you will realize that the 'Charleston' house has been trimmed like a sail whenever it was possible to square against the course of this most favorable breezes." ❧ To this we may add the benefits of a gardening space adjacent to literally every room in the house. And the practicality of separateness, of not having as John Bennett described "the air for one the air for all," of having the leaking roof of one bring "wall ferns" sprouting on its neighbors. And to all of the above, we must add the independent nature of Charlestonians that required each person to be separate from his neighbor, careful to preserve his neighbor's privacy and to expect the same courtesy in return. Naturally, this same sense of individuality affected the houses themselves. Size could run from a cottage to a castle—an alley-bound frame tenement of 1,000 square feet to a "modified" single mansion on the Battery. Greek Revival or Italianate, any "arriving" architectural style could be bent to this purpose, and of course, the pre-Revolutionary

EAST BAY STREET

Built on the last of the city's original high ground, these two offer a good lesson in single house architecture.

houses could be converted to double piazza status. Which returns us to the subject of Charleston's eclectic architectural jumbling charm. ※ Though some neighborhoods do suggest a repetition of house styles, even these can be deceiving. Subtle and not so subtle shifts in roofline and surface and a grand variety of opening treatments add variety. And, of course, the color and texture of the exterior do as well, and to this we might add the ironwork or forests of columns with crowning capitals. Architecture's secret ingredient is detail, and this city has a dizzying amount. ※ And remember, many Charlestonians had no aversion to "modernizing" their buildings. Pre-Revolutionary homes were given Federal mantels. Federal mansions got Greek Revival columns. And Victorian ironwork and mansard roofs could go onto any of the above. All of which may cause today's purists to grumble but still suggests a happy amount of decorative energy churning away.

PATCHES AND LAYERS / *Charleston is a city of patches and layers. Beneath that slate walk lies the crushed shell of an Indian midden. Beneath the concrete, perhaps cobblestone. Beneath that*

stucco is surely brick. And the roofs can be layers of anything under the shining Carolina sun—wood shakes with tiles or an overcoat of standing seam tin. Yes, Charleston has been worn thin in places and put back more than once. She was bombarded with cannons during both the Revolutionary and Civil wars. Often disastrous fires would sweep through the community, destroying everything in their paths. (The Fires of 1692, 1740, 1778, 1796, 1838, and 1861; hurricanes would do the same—Hugo of 1989 being one of the worst.) The low-lying city could easily flood, and the Battery does appear on close inspection to be like the dike of a Dutch town. Rooftops went and an occasional chimney, but tornadoes took those as well. ※ The Earthquake of 1886 was probably the most important "event" for patching up and "layering." Earthquake bolts went long ways through the houses between the floors. We see the nuts and plates on the end. Stucco covered cracked and crumbling brick—sometimes scoured to look like stone and sometimes only on the street facade. But often enough to make us forget that Charleston is a city of brick, some of bright red.

GARDENS / *Charleston was settled by botanizers and horticulturalists. And by gardeners.*

"Their gardens also began to be beautified and adorned with such Herbs and Flowers which to the smell or Eye are pleasing and agreeable, viz: the Rose, Tulip, Carnation and Lilly, Etc.," commented Thomas Ashe in 1682. This dependence on the familiar was an antidote to homesickness, no doubt, but Carolina flowers and shrubs were already being shipped back to avid European collectors. Sea captains would aid in this worldwide transaction—and so would diplomats. Ambassador Joel Poinsett returned from his South American tenure with the Poinsettia. Henry Laurens kept a fine garden, as did the Frenchman Michaux who gave us the camellia and turned out to be a spy. ❧ The gardens of Charleston are a product of happy coincidence. The Gulf Stream gives us the heat of the tropics, which means a long growing season and a tradition of semi-outdoor living. But first it means the presence of live oaks, magnolias, dogwoods, sweet bay, red bud, palmetto, wax myrtle, jessamine, and cassina growing wild—and the ornamental Spanish moss and exploding ferns that are all found in this area's "Florida" maritime forest. So the gardens, even the most formal and "European," impose themselves on a lush and tropical setting. More layering. Humanity proposing and God growing. A layering of leaf and bloom, vigorous domestication-wisteria, tea olive, camellias, azaleas, parkinsonia, roses, jessamine and jasmine, plumbago and oleander, hydrangias, and banana shrub, and hundreds of others. ❧ But an ordering nonetheless. Gardeners were imported along with plants, and the grandest and most formal of houses had large gardens to match—shaped boxwoods and tulip beds of geometric precision, which we see at the Nathaniel Russell house and elsewhere. And outside the city were tremendous landscape gardens like those of Magnolia Gardens and Middleton Place. ❧ Charleston is equally well known for her more intimate and less "historical"

SOUTH BATTERY GARDEN

The gracefully sculpted beds and barrel-vaulted arbor are mimicked in the curve of skillfully crafted iron.

city gardens—those tucked away in sideyards and backyards or any odd corners. Architecture has played its part—especially in the case of the single house—for the houses carry a tradition of open-air living. Ancient walls, built for the purposes of privacy and protection, help to create a sense of enclosure and serenity, as do the gates and fences of finely turned wrought iron; these that offer a glimpse of the haven within set the garden's mood. As does a careful placement of pavings and borders—shell, sand, brick, slate, Belgian blocks, and cobblestones. And, of course, the points of interest are provided by fountains and small statuary. ❧ "Privacy, serenity, enclosure, fragrance, intimacy, beauty, practicality, and genius for detail," writes James Cothran, those are the hallmarks of a small garden tradition, which he dates only from the beginning of this century—at the time when the preservation movement was beginning and the earlier "service" aspects of the yards were being abandoned. They are a happy combination of the formal tradition and the tropical growth—a series of outdoor rooms where every inch is of decorative value, but "living" in the space is of the utmost importance. Modern garden designers like Loutrel Briggs led the way and others have gladly followed. Such gardens can be glimpsed from the sidewalks and enjoyed up close when they're open for tours. "If you have something beautiful, you should share it," says Emily Whaley, local gardener and best-selling author. "Gardens above all else are for sharing."

PRESERVATION / *Many believe that Charleston's fight to save its architectural heritage can be traced largely to one woman, Susan Pringle Frost, suffragette, social conscience, and preservationist par excellence.*

To keep buildings from being razed for business sites and to stop the dismantling of historic interiors by outsiders, she began to buy up buildings in a piecemeal fashion. Her selfless, if somewhat haphazard, real estate dealings would make her the "angel of Tradd Street" and the protector of Church Street, St. Michael's Alley, and the Miles Brewton House. The Preservation Society of Charleston, which she helped to form, saved the Joseph Manigault House and many others. The oldest preservation society in America, this group now watches over zoning ordinances, conducts house and garden tours, works with schools and neighborhood groups to extend the preservation concept in new directions, and more. ❧ In the 1940s, Frances Edmunds began a related effort that systemized and broadened the base of preservation efforts. Her Historic Charleston Foundation was established with a revolving fund that could be used to purchase and restore buildings that would then be resold. The resurrection of the entire Ansonborough neighborhood was its most successful project, and the foundation is now concentrating on renewing other neighborhoods in a manner that

allows the poorer residents to remain. It also runs two museum houses, the Proprietary Period Museum, and the Festival of Houses and Gardens tours. ⁂ The Charleston Museum has a long history of preservation work, as does the city. And all organizations act in conjunction with the city's Board of Architectural Review and various other agencies to create a protective shield over the historic district. Occasionally, architects and homeowners find the procedures stifling, but once removed or altered, a historic building is irreparably harmed. And the true heroes of the preservation effort are, after all, the patient architects and homeowners of Charleston.

A WORD ABOUT WORDS / *Now consider this. Charleston is a place of stories, a construction of words. All of these architectural details—column, cornices, dental molding, roof pitches, window pane*

size—you can learn to "read" them eventually. Of course, the same is true of garden design and the names and habits of plants. And history—who did what and why and how—you can learn that as well. ⁂ But the sight, scent, and sound of the city is immediate. ⁂ But the more you learn and understand, the richer your pleasure will be. ⁂ Take for instance the numerous churches of this Holy City. If we set aside the obvious fact that for many they are God's homes and already filled with His joy, what else can we learn? Before the great fire of 1838, most could be placed in the Wren-Gibbs tradition— that's the grand steepled tradition of St. Michael's and St. Philip's. Then came an

THE BLACKLOCK HOUSE
18 BULL STREET
An intricate low arch over the door is complemented by the bolder one of the attic gable.

epidemic of the Neoclassical temples, and in reaction to these came a return to the more Christian and perpendicular lines of the Gothic. And what else do we know? That the steeples of St. Michael's and St. Philip's have acted as watch-towers and lighthouses; that St. Michael's was painted black to camouflage it from the English King's cannon fire (it stood out worse); and that St. Philip's, it's said, was painted brown when the "brownstone craze" of the mid-18th century swept through. ❧ The earlier St. Philip's, which burned in 1835, extended even farther onto Church Street. Like the Exchange Building at one end of Broad and the missing town square at the other end, the massive portico was meant to block the road entirely and be the commanding centerpiece of the view. Anxious to get started with a replacement, the church members set the new structure back 40 feet to let traffic by and then began construction without a complete plan—so the handsome church we have today is a work-in-progress compromise. ❧ And the bells of St. Michael's. They've been used to give the alarm in case of fire and sound the curfew for slaves. And they announced patriotic meetings, as well as funerals, weddings, and Sunday services. They were cast in England and then stolen back by British forces, then returned, moved to Columbia when Sherman invaded, and shattered when that city fell. The pieces were then returned to England and recast. And that's what you hear ringing today. ❧ But these stories are just the tiniest tip of the historical and architectural iceberg. Much, much more is known of these two churches and who built them and attended them—all the layers that tell us "what happened next." And if we multiply this informa-tion by the number of other churches around, we can begin to understand the true nature of our riches. Charleston is a construction of stories. And Charleston is a treat for the senses—"the sensuous city." ❧ We can see without knowing. We can know without seeing. But how happy we are to both know and see. Enjoy the city.

SOUTH BATTERY HOUSES

A grand line of
"wedding cake" trim graces
the front of some of the
city's most eclectic and most
beautiful architecture.

AIKEN-RHETT HOUSE / 48 ELIZABETH STREET

Unrestored and elegant in its shabbiness, this mammoth

Federal double house is open to the public. Brick for brick, it has to be

the most unreconstructedly romantic spot in the city.

CALHOUN MANSION / VIEW OF ROOFTOPS

Rooftops sculpted by hurricane, earthquake, tornado,

and cannonballs. But they seem serene enough now with all that

treetop accompaniment.

OLD COURT HOUSE / 84 BROAD STREET

"It is content to be big, solid, square, and lofty, serving its

purposes and making no fuss," observed William Gilmore Simms. There's some

"fuss" surrounding its preservation, but all concerned hold

the 1753 edifice in reverence.

DOCK STREET THEATRE / 135 CHURCH STREET

Famed for its cuisine, the old Planter's Hotel probably gave

Planter's punch to the world. Between 1933 and 1936, the New Deal pumped

$34 million into Charleston County, and a bit of that went into

restoring the derelict building as a public theatre.

CATFISH ROW'S PORGY / 83-85 CHURCH

Goat-cart beggar Sammy Smalls was the source of Dubose Heyward's

novel character Porgy. *Actually called Cabbage Row for the vegetable on sale, Heyward changed it*

to Catfish. In real life, a porgy is a small and tasty saltwater fish. "Porgy walk, Porgy talk,

Porgy eat with knife and fork," sang the fish peddlers of that day. An inspired Heyward

and Gershwin came up with a true American opera, Porgy and Bess.

RAINBOW ROW / 83-108 EAST BAY

These dozen-plus houses constitute Rainbow Row, so named for the

rainbow of pastel colors applied during restoration in the 1930s. Most of the

structures date from just after the Revolution and had shops on the

bottom and living quarters above.

SWEET GRASS BASKETS

For sale at the Market, on sidewalks, and at highway stands, these

sweet grass baskets are closely related to rush baskets made by rice-growing

African slaves, for the craft has been passed down from them

to skilled Gullah descendants. A great bargain. Baskets exactly

like these are exhibited in museums all over America.

THE BATTERY

This world-class promenade began as a much humbler

defense against hurricanes and enemy invasion. The statue celebrates the

Confederate defenders of Fort Sumter. Look closely. There's nothing between

you and the Canary Islands but a lone jogger and that fort.

HIBERNIAN HALL
105 MEETING STREET
*Built by an Irish benevolent
society whose 1840
dedication celebration incited
an impromptu dance. The
St. Cecilia Society balls are
still held here and so is the
St. Patrick's Day celebration.*

KRESS BUILDING / 281 KING STREET

Edward Sibbert, designer of over 200 Kress dime stores, was a master

of the Art Deco vocabulary. Though always working in butterscotch-colored

tiles, he borrowed motifs from the neighbors. Here the bracketed

columns and indented windows receive a Charleston

Neoclassical/Cubist flourish.

RIVIERA THEATRE / 227 KING STREET

The whimsy of Art Deco helped to lighten the grimness of the

Great Depression. And so did the movies. When this theater opened in 1939,

it seated 1,200 "escaping" moviegoers, but it's converted

now to shops and a convention center.

CITY HALL WITH ANGEL GABRIEL

Architect Gabriel Manigault left his signature, this little

Angel Gabriel on City Hall—unless that's just a generic

"goddess of victory" as some spoilsports claim. High in the

pediment, the city's seal declares, "She guards her customs,

her buildings, and her laws."

STOREFRONTS / 209-235 MEETING STREET

The use of cast-iron storefronts increased the size of the glass

display windows and allowed for sturdier construction.

This was state-of-the-art architecture in the 1850s, the

same techniques that would make the Chicago skyscrapers

possible a few decades later. But Charleston was going

through hard times by then.

FIRE INSURANCE PLAQUE

Just five years after the first fire insurance company in

America was formed here, the fire of 1740 claimed 300

houses. With closely built houses, many of wood, Charleston

was always in danger of burning down, so insurance

companies placed these distinctive markers on the buildings

they were contracted to save.

AVERY INSTITUTE / 125 BULL STREET

This was the 1867 home of Charleston's first free

secondary school for blacks, and for decades it provided

first-rate education. Absorbed into the public school

system, it now houses a research center and museum

and is open to the public.

ASHLEY HALL / 172 RUTLEDGE AVENUE

A Regency Villa designed by Savannah architect William Jay

was home to Confederate treasurer George Trenholm

(thought to be the model of blockade-running Rhett Butler).

The conch-lined house was German banker Otto Witte's

aviary. His daughter Laura Waring tells of not just birds,

but a vast menagerie of animals living on the grounds.

The girls' school Ashley Hall began its tenacy in 1909.

COLLEGE OF CHARLESTON / MAIN BUILDING

Air flowing through the large windows of the College of

Charleston building was to bring 19th-century students

"to more vigorous mental exercise, as well as to more healthful

action of bodily powers." The dome housed a telescope.

The cistern in front is a modern-day resting place for

those vigorously seeking even more fresh air.

RICE MILL ON ASHLEY RIVER

"Skill, imagination and planning," wrote Frances Edmunds.

That's what made adaptive architecture work. Built in

1860, the West Point Rice Mill was renovated by the WPA

and is now used by the city marina.

COLONIAL LAKE

An artificial lake was created here on a tidal flat.

Back when this was called "the pond," rowboating courters

navigated and serenaded. Today's joys are limited to

the oleander-lined perimeter.

BLUESTEINS

CORNER OF KING AND MARY STREETS

Upper King Street is sprucing up. John Maher

recalled in the 1920s that a fine man's suit could be bought

here for $12.50. "Broad Street is recognized as the

Head of the City," he said, "but one could scarcely deny

that King Street is its Heart."

FIREPROOF BUILDING

100 MEETING STREET

Architect Robert Mills used elements of both Greek and

Roman architecture for this County Records Building and

set the stage for dozens of public "temples" built in

Charleston before the Civil War. Incidentally, the structure is

just fire resistant not fireproof. Peculiar to Charleston, the

peppermint peach tree adds splashes of both pink and white.

WATERFRONT PARK

"Autothalassous" may be the Greek word that fits. A city

sprung from the sea. Or if you prefer Lee Robinson's

version, "Water is everywhere, shining and silvery. Water is

what will stay." In the meantime, this new park is being

eagerly embraced by residents and tourists alike.

VISITORS CENTER / MEETING STREET

The antebellum dream was to improve Charleston's

sagging economy by connecting her to the Mississippi by

rail. Not much came of it, though. To protect the residential

neighborhoods, trains were allowed to come no closer to

the wharves than this Mary Street warehouse, which

now serves as the city's Visitors Center.

HERON FOUNTAIN BEHIND POST OFFICE

This dancing heron has found a home in front of the new

Hollings Judicial Center. The true-to-life flock of yellow-crowned night

herons that has invaded Washington Park just beyond the church

isn't quite so welcome, except by bird-watchers.

EAST BATTERY HOUSES AT SUNRISE

It was predicted that the sale of these new "made" lots would

produce "a beautiful row of ornamental buildings." And between

1820 and 1850 that's exactly what happened. It's a romantic

spectacle at any time of day, but especially when the sun rises.

POWDER HOUSE
HURRICANE BOLT
*Following the devastating
earthquake of 1886,
Charleston was literally bolted
back together with long rods
that ran the widths of the
buildings. This one graces the
Powder House, home of the
Proprietary Period Museum.*

CALHOUN MANSION FRONT HALL

The golden wall covering is a popular marbleizing—"faux marbre."

The trim is mahogany with satinwood inlay of cloverleafs to signify the

Holy Trinity. And just for good measure, the griffins and lions

in the tiles of the ceiling guard against evil spirits.

CALHOUN MANSION / 16 MEETING STREET

This Victorian residence was built by banker and philanthropist

George Walton Williams just after the Civil War. With 24,000 square feet,

it's the biggest residence in the city. Williams' daughter married John C.

Calhoun's grandson, Patrick, and this was their home until the stock

market crash in 1929. The house then served as a hotel before being

rescued and restored. Open to the public as a museum house.

NATHANIEL RUSSELL HOUSE LIBRARY

One of three elliptical rooms, this handsome library boasts globes by Carry,

and on the table is an edition of the works of Palliadio. Above the mantle is a

portrait of Nathaniel Russell painted by Edward Savage.

NATHANIEL RUSSELL HOUSE / 51 MEETING STREET

Built by "the King of the Yankees," this 1809 mansion boasts quite fashionable

red brick and white stone trim. The elegant garden complements the formality of the house with

blooming Camellia japonica, azaleas, and trimmed boxwood hedges surrounding

a bed of tulips. Both the garden and the house are open to the public.

EDMONDSTON-ALSTON HOUSE LIBRARY

The books in this library haven't left it since they were acquired. The harbor view provided by

that window suggests the old Beaufort poem might apply: "One had to have a library, One loved

to have a boat." But with a library this comfortable, perhaps just the opposite was true.

EDMONDSTON-ALSTON HOUSE / 21 EAST BATTERY

Finished in 1828, this Regency-style mansion was built by merchant Charles Edmonston.

He lost it in a financial panic 10 years later, and rice planter Charles Alston bought it

and added the Greek Revival features. Much of the Alston family's fine furnishings are

still inside. The house is open to the public.

HEYWARD-WASHINGTON HOUSE / 87 CHURCH STREET

"Lodging provided for me in this place were very good, being the

furnished house of a gentleman at present in the country," wrote President

George Washington in 1791. The missing gentleman was Thomas Heyward

Jr., a signer of the Declaration of Independence. Earlier this century, a bakery

was removed from the downstairs and a pool room from the kitchen.

The Charleston Museum opened the restored building to the public.

JOSEPH MANIGAULT HOUSE / 350 MEETING STREET

"One of the perfect pearls on the now loosened string of architectural gems,"

wrote Nell Pringle. Sixty some years ago, room was needed for a gas station

that was to be called "Automobile City," and the house was scheduled

for demolition. Through a valiant effort it was saved, beautifully

restored, and opened to the public.

AIKEN-RHETT
CARRIAGE HOUSE
*Twelve to eighteen slaves
maintained the family and
were quartered in these small
dormitories. Seen through
the window is a carriage
house complete with
dilapidated carriage.*

MILES BREWTON HOUSE / 27 KING STREET

Considered to be Charleston's finest dwelling, the 1769 Palladian

mansion was occupied by General Lord Cornwallis. Following the Civil

War, the Union commander, General Meade, moved in. The Preservation

Society's Susan Pringle Frost lived here in the first half of this century—

when she waged her war to preserve Charleston's architecture.

THOMAS ELFE HOUSE KITCHEN / 54 QUEEN STREET

Best known of the Charleston furniture makers, Thomas Elfe is credited

with over 1,500 handsome pieces. His 1740 home offers a unique

glimpse into a tradesman's life, and it's open to the public. This award-

winning kitchen is a masterpiece in its own right. Look closely

and see if you can spot the modern appliances.

PATRICK O'DONNELL HOUSE

21 KING STREET

O'Donnell's folly. Legend has it that the Irishman

set out to build this outstanding house for his bride to be,

but construction took so long she married someone

else. The wife of a subsequent owner was

the model for Gone with the Wind's *Melanie.*

ROPER HOUSE / 9 EAST BATTERY

The doorway to a monumental single house.

The rope trim surrounding the door symbolizes

great wealth, but here the design may be doing

double duty—it's a "canting" pun on the

owner's name, Robert Roper.

DR. JOHN LINING HOUSE

106 BROAD STREET

This home is one of the earliest frame structures in the city.

It operated as a pharmacy and was the site of the Mermaid

Riots. After rains destroyed crops and brought fevers, it

was rumored that the building held a mermaid. The city's

more superstitious element stormed inside and released

a bottled sea horse. The rains stopped. The apothecary

fittings are now in the Charleston Museum.

RUTLEDGE HOUSE / 116 BROAD STREET

John Rutledge was a member of the South Carolina General

Assembly, the Stamp Act Congress, and the Continental

Congress. He was president of South Carolina during the

Revolution, attended the Constitutional Convention, and

was an associate justice on the U.S. Supreme Court.

The Victorian restoration of this house was done in the

1850s by Charleston architect P.H. Hammerskold.

EVELEIGH HOUSE / 39 CHURCH STREET

Though this Indian trader's home once enjoyed a view of

the creek, the odd posts weren't for tying up boats.

The sidewalks were made of fragile Bermuda stone, which

couldn't stand the weight of carriage wheels.

DENMARK VESEY HOUSE / BULL STREET

In 1822, freed slave Denmark Vesey was hanged for

attempting to lead a slave insurrection. The plan was to rise

up, murder as many white people as possible, and flee on

ships to the safe haven of Haiti. Perhaps AME Bishop Frank

Reid Jr. put it best: "We know who Denmark Vesey was

and we know who we are. We know what he intended to

do to them and we know what they did to him."

The front third of the building dates from Vesey's residency.

STUDIO OF ELIZABETH O'NEILL VERNER

38-40 TRADD STREET

"Seething with vermin, and great wharf rats" said

Verner of this neighborhood. "Typhoid was prevalent

and bedbugs a curse." But her etchings captured only the

charm, and that's all that remains today.

DEWAR-LEE-PRINGLE HOUSE

92 TRADD STREET

Antebellum home of the free black hotel owners John and

Eliza Seymour Lee. They gave this house a Greek and

Egyptian Revival makeover and ran the Jones Hotel—

"the finest inn in the place," as described by a

19th-century traveler.

PINK HOUSE / 17 CHALMERS STREET

Built around 1712, this "Old World Refugee" is probably

the city's earliest house. Set ground level with thick walls of

coral and brick, small windows, large chimney, and tiled

gambrel roof, it demonstrates an imported building tradition.

Before the Revolution, it was a tavern serving free-spending

sailors. The Old World cobblestones surfacing the street

were brought by ships—ballast in the holds that would be

jettisoned when a New World cargo came aboard.

C H A R L E S T O N

PIRATE HOUSE / 143-145 CHURCH STREET

This 1740 Bermuda stone dwelling got an extensive restoration in 1928—and

at that late date picked up the legend of pirate occupants. It's true Charleston had

tolerated and even entertained pirates, but after Stede Bonnet and his compan-

ions were hanged in 1718, pirates tended to give Charleston a wide berth. The

window boxes contain gerbers, salvia, dusty miller, lantana, and creeping ficus.

CONFEDERATE HOME COURTYARD / 60 BROAD STREET

This building served as a residence, department store, and hotel

before becoming "The Home for the Widows and Daughters of Confederate

Soldiers and Sailors." The Broad Street facade "seemed clasped in some

iron-clad bitterness," wrote Harlan Greene. But once inside, there was

the tree, "waving in front of us, green and dazzling."

MIKELL HOUSE & GARDEN
94 RUTLEDGE AVENUE

Sea Island cotton planter
I. Jenkins Mikell built this
Italian villa for his bride in
1853. From 1936 to 1960, it
served as the county library and
then was handsomely restored.
Clipped boxwood complement
the Neoclassical facade.

ENTRANCE ON EAST BATTERY

This graceful spiraling grill or clairvoyee draws in the eye and

offers a teasing view of the quiet within.

SWORD GATE / 32 LEGARE STREET

Two spears, the points of which join at the center of a broad sword to

form a cross. Ironworker Christopher Werner accidentally made two sets for

the city's Guard House, so the second set came here. And as a fashionable

girl's school, it's said that the high fence went up after a particularly

romantic elopee or eloper carried off one of the girls.

DOGS ON A PORCH

Father and son. Or is this mother and child? Anyway, here's a clear case of adventurous

youth suspecting that there just might be more to life than a front porch.

KITCHEN DEPENDENCY ON ANSON STREET / 63 ANSON

Kitchens were separated from the main houses as a protection from fire and the

odors of cooking. But these days their intimate scale makes them comfortable homes.

Begun in 1958, rehabilitation of Ansonborough is among the most successful

undertakings of the Historic Charleston Foundation.

VICTORIAN / 40 MONTAGU STREET

Charleston did enjoy a decade or two of postbellum prosperity, and some Victorian beauties

did get built. This one's been labeled a mixture of Queen Anne, Eastlake, and Shingle styles, but

then Charlestonians have never been reluctant to mix and match when the mood struck.

ENTRANCE ALLEY ON WATER STREET

The hard lines of a narrow entry are easily gentled by these overflowing ferns.

Though the official marker is over by White Point Garden, it's thought that Stede Bonnet

and his pirate brethren were hanged right about here.

WINDOW BOXES ON QUEEN STREET

A predictable feature of many Charleston streetscapes—houses pressed

against the sidewalk. So here's a happy compromise between slate or

concrete and Mother Nature. Ferns in window boxes.

A GILLON STREET WINDOW BOX

Window boxes, a Charleston institution, are perfect for squeezing

out every inch of garden space. This one on shady Gillon Street is planted

with snapdragons, vinca, and cyclamen.

ISAAC MOTTE
DART HOUSE
54 MONTAGU STREET

*Though Dart was a factor
and attorney, his 1809 single
house is reminiscent of
plantation architecture.
In the far distance is a view
of the Avery Institute.*

GARDEN THROUGH IRON GATE ON CHURCH

A broad expanse of pink stucco and the swirling tendrils of a black iron gate.

Charleston's wrought-iron tradition makes a bold "American" use of

ancient imported designs.

THE THREE SISTERS / 90 CHURCH STREET AND NEIGHBORS

Three handsome single houses speak volumes. The northernmost house dates

from 1730, the southernmost from 1760. Only the 1809 middle structure was

built with a piazza originally, and it was placed in the garden of the first.

Doors, windows, and lifestyles shifted accordingly.

JAMES VEREE HOUSE GARDEN

"A walled garden to keep out the lions and tigers."

Mrs. Emily Whaley's retreat is a well-known spot,

for it's a favorite of garden tours and the subject

of a wonderful memoir.

SIDE GARDEN ON CHURCH STREET

Small statuary pays dividends in a small garden.

Frogs, cats, birds, even whimsical pigs are enshrined

by Charleston gardeners.

ROSES ON TRADD STREET

A glossy leaf Cherokee rose (Rosa laevigala)

"clothes" the garden wall.

GARDEN OF VANDERHORST ROW HOUSE

76-78 EAST BAY STREET

This long, narrow garden facing the Cooper River

is designed as a series of three outdoor rooms, each

with a different emphasis.

GARDEN AND PLAYHOUSE

(SHACKLEFORD WMS.)

Hidden in the depth of this oasis is a 1903 playhouse.

Built with tongue-and-groove paneling and boasting a

tiny crystal chandelier, the little structure has in years

since served as clubhouse and garden shed. The Hallmark

Company used the image on its Easter card last year.

CAT ON A RAIL

A fine place to wile away nine lives—or even one.

PORCH AND ENTRY OF GARDEN

ON CHURCH.

Making the most of a typical narrow entry yard,

the bed contains snapdragons, calendulas, pansies,

and sweet alyssum.

ISAAC MAZYCK HOUSE GARDEN

A bit of bright green to rest the eye.

CALHOUN MANSION GARDEN GATE

FOR THE CARRIAGE HOUSE

A near perfect palette. Pink stucco, gray slate,

black iron, green grass, and just a splash of sun-colored

Lady Banksia roses.

HANGING BASKETS ON CHURCH STREET

The beautiful baskets full of spring bloomers, including

pansies and sweet alyssum, hang from both levels of

the piazza. Espaliered pyracantha forms patterns on

the dividing wall and Carolina jasmine, the state

flower, is trained on the gate.

BENJAMIN SIMMONS NEUFVILLE HOUSE

THE GARDEN

The big-leafed Acanthus mollis in the foreground and unusual

sedum in pots surrounding the shallow pond hint at the uniqueness

of this plant woman's garden.

ELLIOT STREET SMALL GARDEN

The brick walls of these yards were built originally to provide

security and privacy and to contain livestock, but they lend themselves

well to garden planning.

PINEAPPLE GATE

14 LEGARE STREET

*The owners ordered a set
of marble live oak acorns
from Italy, but they were
sent Mediterranean "pine
cone" finials instead. And
these are mistaken today
for that old symbol of
welcome, pineapples.*

ANGEL OAK / JOHN'S ISLAND

The old saying is that "A live oak grows for a hundred years,

lives for a hundred years, and dies for a hundred years."

That makes the Angel Oak the Methuselah of oaks, for it's been

doing all three for at least a thousand. Open to the public.

MIDDLETON PLACE / HWY 61

Laid out in 1741, Middleton Place boasts America's oldest

landscape gardens—as well as terraced lawns, "butterfly"

lakes, an authentic antebellum stable yard, and museum

house. "More than a garden," wrote garden enthusiast

E.T.H. Shaffer, "a little world."

DRAYTON HALL / HWY 61

One of the finest examples of colonial architecture in

America. When this Palladian Mansion was built in 1740,

the frontier of the colony was practically at its door. And it's

the only such mansion on the Ashley River to survive

the ravages of Yankee soldiers and Southern time.

Maintained by the National Trust for Historic Preservation,

it's open to the public.

CYPRESS GARDENS / HWY 52

Already famed for its cypress-crowded blackwater ponds and grand gardens, Cypress Gardens is now home to a butterfly barn and accompanying nature trails. Incidentally, that's not a butterfly. It's a silk moth. The Chinese and early Carolinians used its domesticated cousin to manufacture silk.

FORT SUMTER

Here's the little fort that started the big war. Actually, the South fired first. But the North got in the final winning salvo, so it's a United States national park today and not the useless pile of rubble that we left behind.

MAGNOLIA GARDENS / HWY 61

Travel writer/newsman Charles Kuralt called Magnolia "my greatest Charleston pleasure." Visitors have been saying that about Rev. John Grimke Drayton's "Romantic" garden for over 150 years. And now there's a new Audubon Swamp Garden to add to the pleasure.

THE NATIONAL PARK SERVICE

BOONE HALL MT. PLEASANT / HWY 17 N.

These nine brick slave quarters are listed on the

National Register. There are guided tours of the plantation

house, gin house, gardens, and an almost endless

live oak avenue.

MAGNOLIA CEMETERY

This 1850s "City of the Dead" was modeled on the then-new

European concept of cemetery as park. Many of Charleston's

Confederate dead lie here entombed, as does the winning coach

of the first Clemson-Carolina football game.

CHARLES TOWNE LANDING

"God will preserve me as he hath in many great dangers

when I saw his wonders on ye Deepe & was by him

Delivered," wrote a survivor of the first voyage. The colonists

arrived in vessels hardly larger than this one and

laid claim to this beautiful little corner of Carolina.

The Landing is run as a state park.

FORT MOULTRIE / SULLIVAN'S ISLAND

On the eve of the American Revolution,

a critic referred to the fort's palmetto log and sand

embankments as "a slaughter pen." But the defenders

prevailed against the British navy's finest. During the heat

of battle, Sergeant William Jasper rescued our fallen flag

from the rampart, and afterward the palmetto was added

to the crescent of the blue background banner.

PATRIOTS POINT

FLIGHT DECK OF THE YORKTOWN

In the beginning, the harbor anchorage just to the

seaward was called "Rebellion Road," for a ship anchored

there was beyond the reach of the city's guns. These jet

fighters on the deck of the aircraft carrier Yorktown *had a*

bit more range. Also docked here are a submarine, a

destroyer, and a nuclear-powered freighter. Below deck of

the carrier is a hangar filled with historic aircraft.

One of Charleston's most popular attractions.

SHEM CREEK SHRIMP BOATS

Shrimp trawlers in port. Just lower the outriggers and

"bail out the mess." Well, it's not all that easy, and at day's

end "to the piling" is a fine place to be.

...ies Inter'd the body of

ELIZABETH HOLMES

Mr ISAAC HOLMES Junr.

...hter of Mr Joseph

In Memory of Mr ISAAC HOLMES
of Charlstown Merchant

He _____ ender Husband, an affectionate Pa

an indulgent Master & a sincere Christian

He departed this Life the 17th Day of December

Aged 34 Years

And of SUSANNA HOLMES his youngest Daug

who Lies interr'd in the Same Grave She depar

this Life 11th Day of April 1763 Aged 9 M

**CONGREGATIONAL
CHURCHYARD
A PORTRAIT
GRAVESTONE**

*Stone was a rarity in early
Carolina, so the earliest grave
markers were often of wood.
But by the beginning of the
18th century, some stones
were imported to Charleston.*

ST. MICHAEL'S CHURCH BAPTISMAL FONT

An object of beauty placed here on Christmas eve of 1771.

"It was to stand upon a mahogany frame, run upon brass casters, and

not exceed the price of ten guineas," wrote the vestry. The dove

is of lead and balances the font cover.

ST. STEPHEN'S CHURCH / 67 ANSON STREET

St. Stephen's has established a niche in Charleston's spiritual landscape. A truly

integrated and open-minded congregation meets here for a conservative "high

church" Episcopal ceremony. "If your chief object in going to church is to keep

in the swim socially. ... St. Stephen's is not the place for you." This 19th-century

admonition is still true today. Lady Banksia roses and dogwood bless the front.

FIRST SCOTS PRESBYTERIAN CHURCH

53 MEETING STREET

In 1731, a group of "Scots Kirk" Presbyterians broke

from the Congregationalist Church up the street and built

here. The present church dates from 1814. The distinctive

twin bell towers hold only "ghost bells," for the bells were

melted down during the Civil War to make cannons.

FIRST BAPTIST CHURCH

61 CHURCH STREET

This site was deeded to the "antipaedobaptist" congrega-

tion in 1699. And a "Baptist town" church has been here

ever since. Lord Cornwallis claimed he feared the prayers

of the young Baptist minister Richard Furman "more than

the armies of Marion and Sumter." Furman founded

Furman University. Architect Robert Mills designed the

present 1822 structure and called it, in all modesty, "the

best specimen of correct taste in architecture of all the

modern buildings in this city." Others agree.

CONGREGATIONAL CHURCH

150 MEETING STREET

In 1681, Congregationalists built their

"White Meeting House" on this site. Hence the name

Meeting Street. This Romanesque Revival building

dates from only 1890, but the ancient previously

used brick and antique design bestow on the

newcomer a solid sense of belonging.

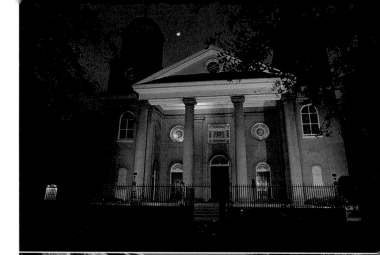

HUGUENOT CHURCH / 136 CHURCH STREET

The Huguenots, French Protestants fleeing persecution, built on this site in 1687. But this 1844 structure was actually to serve an Episcopal congregation that decided to return to its French roots. The Gothic style was a churchman's revolt against the pagan associations of the popular Neoclassical lines being used by others.

MOUNT ZION AME CHURCH
7 GLEBE STREET

Designed by Francis Lee when he was only 21, this distinctive building was for a Presbyterian congregation, which then relinquished it in 1882. The tower has been referred to, perhaps unkindly, as a sarcophagus, but Lee was an absolute master of the exotic—even at 21.

BETH ELOHIEM SYNAGOGUE
90 HASSELL STREET

"This synagogue is our 'temple,' this city our 'Jerusalem,' this happy land our 'Palestine'" wrote an 18th-century rabbi. By 1800, Charleston had the largest Jewish population of any city in the country. "Floor space was maximized," comments architectural historian Gene Waddell, and "an impression of even greater spaciousness than actually exists was achieved in part by inserting a saucer dome fifty feet in diameter."

UNITARIAN CHURCH AND LUTHERAN CHURCH

ARCHDALE STREET

Built under the direction of pastor John Bachman in 1816, this Lutheran Church

boasts fine ironwork by Jacob Roh. Bachman went on to collaborate with painter

James J. Audubon on two of his books. Not to be outdone, Reverend Samuel Gilman next

door at the Unitarian Church had already written the Harvard alma mater.

CATHEDRAL OF *ST.* JOHN THE BAPTIST

122 BROAD STREET

The inspiration for this late 19th-century cathedral was the

14th-century German Gothic. Though many believe that the art of

stained glass has been declining since the Middle Ages, that's hard to

accept when you're in the presence of these radiant Biblical figures.

ST. PHILIP'S CHURCH
146 CHURCH STREET
*"Through all the changes and
chances of this mortal life …
the congregation of St. Philips
… have shared with their
fellow citizens the vicissitudes
of an eventful history," goes
a sermon preached after the
earthquake of 1886.*

AN INFORMAL BIBLIOGRAPHY / A tremendous

amount has been written about Charleston. And besides the

obvious sources of bookstores and conventional libraries, we

have the practically unlimited resources of the Charleston

Library Society and the South Carolina Historical Society.

The fictional works used and sometimes quoted here are Jo

Humphreys' *Dreams of Sleep*; John Bennett's *The Doctor to the Dead*; Harlan Greene's *Why We Never Danced the Charleston*; Josephine

Pinckney's *Three O'Clock Dinner*; Lee Robinson's *Gateway*; Owen Wister's *Lady Baltimore*; and DuBose Heyward's *Porgy*.

The nonfiction works used most often but not exclusively are George C. Rogers Jr.'s *Charleston in the Age of the Pinckneys*; Walter J.

Fraser, Jr.'s *Charleston! Charleston!*; Sam Stoney and the Carolina Art Association's *This is Charleston*; Mrs. St. Julien Ravenel's *Charleston:*

The Place and Her People; Alice Ravenel Huger Smith and D.E. Smith's *The Dwelling Houses of Charleston, South Carolina*; the WPA's

South Carolina: A Guide to the Palmetto State; Jack Leland and William A. Jordon's *Sixty Famous Houses of Charleston, South Carolina*;

Bernard E. Powers Jr.'s *Black Charlestonians*; Sam Stoney's *Charleston: Azaleas and Old Bricks*; Albert Simons and S. Lapham, Jr.'s *The*

Early Architecture of Charleston; Mills Lane's *Architecture of the Old South: South Carolina*; Kenneth Severens's *Charleston: Antebellum*

Architecture and Civic Destiny; Sidney R. Bland's *Preserving Charleston's Past, Shaping its Future: The Life and Times of Susan Pringle Frost*;

Harriette Kershaw Leiding's *Charleston Historic and Romantic*; Beatrice St. Julien Ravenel's *Architects of Charleston*; Vernacular

Architecture Forum's *The Vernacular Architecture of Charleston and the Lowcountry*; Gene Waddell's *Charleston in 1883*; John Edward

Maher's *An Old Timer's Memories of Charleston*; Elizabeth O'Neill Verner's *Mellowed by Time*; E.T.H. Shaffer's *Carolina Gardens*; Robert

N.S. Whitelaw and Alice F. Levkoff's *Charleston Come Hell or High Water*; H. Roy Merrens' *The Colonial South Carolina Scene*;

Evangeline Davis and N. Jane Iseley's *Charleston Houses and Gardens*; Harlan Greene and N. Jane

Iseley's *Charleston City of Memory*; Tourism Commission's *Information for Guides of Historic*

Charleston; James R. Cothran's *Gardens of Historic Charleston*; Loutrel Briggs' *Charleston Gardens*;

and Emily Whaley and William Baldwin's *Mrs. Whaley and Her Charleston Garden*.

THE EXCHANGE BUILDING
Eliza Lucas introduced indgo
production to the colony.
And to promote locally made
silk, she made this dress.